the last polar bear on earth

Rhian Elizabeth

Parthian, Cardigan SA43 1ED www.parthianbooks.com
First published in 2018
© Rhian Elizabeth 2018
ISBN 978-1-912109-47-0
Editor: Susie Wild
Cover design by Torben Schacht
Typeset by Alison Evans
Printed by Lightning Source
Published with the financial support of the Welsh Books Council
British Library Cataloguing in Publication Data
A cataloguing record for this book is available from the British Library.

contents

disabled single mother

it would not persuade you to swipe right
i know
but i can take you out for sushi and pay
because i got my benefit money through
i can love you the same
as anyone else
can do.

the neurologist

i have loads of lesions
he says
a disease that attacks my brain
hacks away at my spinal cord
like a lumberjack thrashing his axe
into the trunk of a tree
that's fine
i tell him
i'm okay with that
i'm really brave
or really relieved
i was worried about his machine
that in that white tunnel
that click clicks like a typewriter
he'd scanned my brain and saw things
no neurologist should see
old lesions caused by love
internet porn
and secrets
by childhood memories
and brand new scars
that the steroids he prescribed me
won't even heal.

joan baez

nasa found
those other planets in the solar system
i stay up late and watch the news
wondering if there is any chance
that somewhere out there
there is another life
i don't really care that those planets
orbit
a star
if their surfaces
potentially support
liquid water
i just want to know
does love exist there?
do they have dating websites
where aliens can log on
and search for other aliens?
and is it as difficult there
as it is here
to find another alien
who likes the same things you do?
listening to old joan baez records
you find in the market
watching pornographic movies
when the news isn't as interesting
as it is tonight
do they even know who joan baez is there?
and are there aliens
as weird as me?

lupe vélez

once upon a time in hollywood
there was a mexican spitfire
who stormed the stages of broadway
and the silver screen
she was loud and wild
she liked to lift up her skirt
she hated marlene dietrich
and one time she tried to shoot her lover
you don't get the name spitfire
unless you are strong
but her heart was weak
and it got broken
so she decided to poison herself
at dinner that night
she laughed with her friends
and afterwards
adorned her apartment with candles
freshly cut flowers
put on her make-up
her best blue satin pyjamas
and flung herself dead on the bed
i think about this a lot
if someone ever broke my heart
i would definitely want to die too
i'd like to die a spitfire though
just like lupe vélez.

say something about yourself

i like to think of myself
as interesting
i have been to university
i mostly got drunk
and to be honest
i didn't learn a thing
i like movies especially
ones where the world ends
and somebody important dies
but i'm not a film director
if i was i would never kill you off
i like to think of myself
as reasonably attractive
i have blue eyes and black hair
i honestly rarely really brush it
i like music especially
artists who lived
a tragic life and died young
but i'm not a weirdo
i would never croak it and leave you behind
i like to think of myself
as funny
i tell jokes that cause offence
i don't know when to stop
i like girls especially
ones who look as good as you
i swear i've not said that
to any of the others
and i'd really like to fuck.

junaluska

my online dating profile said i was a catch
which was true
if you happened to find
at the end of your rod
a tin can
all folded up
sunk for years at the bottom of that lake.

the train journey that no one else ever took

let me imagine us together
let me think of us on a train journey
i'll let you sit in the window seat
let me lean across you
breathe my breath onto the glass
i'll immortalise you in condensation
let me have something expensive
off the buffet cart
i'll go all out because people in love
can order
anything
they want
let me start up a game to alleviate
the boredom
i'll think of dirty answers for i-spy
let me read you the newspaper
i'll check our horoscopes to see
if our star signs collide
let me prove to you i'm smart
i'll make all the crossword answers
your name
let me snooze on your shoulder when i'm sleepy
i'll say i like the feel
of your cardigan
on my cheek
let me listen to my music
i'll give you an earphone
tell you that i love you more
than joan baez
let us never get off this train
ride on it until
all the other passengers
have alighted

at their stations
let us keep on going until
we end up somewhere
no one else has ever been.

special

i was practical about things at first
in fact i took a morbid interest
i stopped going out with my friends
made a new pal in google
and got excited about letters
inviting me on dates with neurologists
i marked them out on the calendar
impatiently waiting for the next chance
to piss into a cardboard pot
to get chemical dye injected into my veins
for the magnetic resonance scans
keener still to see the photographs
of my brain that they took
as if they were images
of especially arousing porn
i never cried over my brain inflaming
wasn't afraid of my spinal cord eroding
whoever got their heart broken
by damaged sheaths of myelin?
not me i never lost any sleep
over my nerve endings being torched
like letters from old lovers
and i easily forgave my immune system
for attacking the good stuff in my body
like a violent
and abusive
mother
my own cried when i told her the news
her baby was sick
but she needn't have bothered
her baby just felt kind of
special.

hunger strike

i didn't eat in front of you
for the first three months
i wanted you to associate me
with romantic and pretty things
like vintage polaroid cameras
old kodachrome slides
like dark red wax seals on the backs
of envelopes
cows may chomp unapologetically
on a feast of grass in a field
and pigs will guzzle
nose deep in the sludge spilling
from troughs
but that was not going to be me
i was going to be the feeling you get
when the lights go down in the cinema
and that movie you've been wanting to see
for months and months
is about to start
i wasn't going to be the sound of wet
spaghetti slapping against a cheek
or the brazen crunch of a crusty bread roll
my stomach rumbled the whole three months
but i was going to be
the sound of the chorus
of your favourite song
playing on repeat
on repeat.

all these things i think about in the mri machine

this machine is like a prop
from a hollywood movie set in space
a ship sent out into the stars
i could be an astronaut
swap this paper-thin gown
for a spacesuit
i'd love to be blasted up
into
the stratosphere
instead they just leave me in here
flat on my back
while they photograph my brain
like this is its first day at school
will they see this on the computer?
how
on those black and white images
my brain has turned into a planet
and all those lesions
have become craters
lying in this narrow white tube
that could be a coffin
i now know that i want to be cremated
it's weird
how your own body can turn on you
like a dog
who was once your loyal friend
went mad
and ripped off your face
the radiologist is laughing behind the glass
someone must've said something funny
or maybe it was me
can she see them on the computer?

all these things i think about
in the mri machine
i can see her in the tiny mirror
they put in here
to let you know you aren't alone.

i am the moon

i am the moon
and you are the earth
i stare at you constantly
from 384 thousand kilometres away
you are big
and i am small
but i light up your sky
if it's only at night
the sun takes up most of your time
she's my yellow nemesis
but i know you look at me too
if it's only at night
i am always there
but it sucks that i have to share you
with the northern lights
which i admit are more magnificent than me
and also with the stars in their millions
that people wish upon
that now and again shoot
just to show off
and i know no one ever wishes upon a moon
but i don't mind
because if it's only at night
you are mine.

a satellite message to the earth from the moon

neil armstrong came to visit me
on a rocket ship back in the 60s
he took off his helmet and said
that you had been wondering
how i felt under foot
and in your lungs
some say it never happened
that it was staged
in a top-secret movie studio
somewhere real secluded back
in the usa
but he did come he took
some of my rocks away for examination
my gifts to you like diamonds
and pearls
he had brought along a message
scribbled on the back
of the star-spangled banner
the message said that you had claimed me
for your own
and then he went
and rammed it into my surface
like an arrow through my hard
volcanic
heart.

i don't believe in god

it's because i can't handle the thought
of heaven
or hell
and thinking that when i die
i will get sent someplace
i imagine it's like a waiting room
on a train station platform
there are green metal seats
and all the people
i've ever loved
and lost
are there
watching
the screen on the wall
but instead of alerting them
to incoming trains
the screen shows them arrival times
for dead relatives
i flash up but
what would i say to my father?
i'm not the kid he remembers
the kid who sang along with him
to joan baez
the kid who made him proud
because she finally got
that fifty metres swimming badge
or because she made the school quiz team
my grandparents wouldn't recognise me
nan especially
she always held me up on a pedestal
but how could i look her in the eye now?
they're all waiting for me
and then i'm there

15

through the door with my suitcase containing
all the things i've ever achieved in my life
but the zips are bursting with the weight
of all my mistakes.

the girl who cried wolf

when i was a weird kid
i always wanted to be ill
i was jealous of the boys
with plastered arms
that the girls signed their names on
in different coloured felts
i was jealous of the kid in class
with a hearing aid
and the one in the wheelchair
who was allowed straight to the front
of the dinner queue
i thought that girl with the brain tumour
was so lucky
zooming up and down
on my grandfather's stairlift
pretending i was crippled
by a disease i invented
was my favourite game to play
and once i stole his crutches while he slept
convinced my teacher that beneath my tights
the bandage i'd stuck on with sellotape
hid
a mangled leg
now i am sitting in reception
at the neurology clinic
twenty-eight years old
and i really am ill i swear
so i think it's true
that thing they say
if you want something bad enough
you'll get it.

a good mother

when my daughter was four years old
and behaving well
i let her pick a toy
from the shop on the high street
i think it was a mouse she chose
or maybe a rat
anyway it was pink and soft and fluffy
and she treated it like it was real
she called her baby
baby
she was a good mother
fed it with her plastic spoons
tucked it in at night
and slept with it
in the mornings she would take it to school
she couldn't bear to be without her baby
all day long
but one morning when we got to the gates
baby was gone
it had fallen out somewhere along the way
slid through buttons and fabric
the tears went down her cheeks
i had never seen her cry like that
her screams startled the other mothers
she didn't want to go in to school
but i promised
i'd find her baby
i retraced our route a hundred times
because i knew how she felt
or at least i could imagine
what it would feel like
to lose her
it was nowhere though

so i replaced her baby
with the exact same one
from the high street shop
same colour and everything
but somehow
like any good mother
she knew
she did not want to feed the substitute
with her plastic spoons
she left it to starve up on her bedroom shelf
she would not let me tuck her in that night
or kiss her
she turned her wet cheek to the pillow
and i cried
because i was sorry i could not find her baby
i thought maybe if i did
for once i would feel
like a good mother too.

kansas

you are obsessed with *the wizard of oz*
and because i am obsessed with you
i re-write the movie each time i watch it
the scarecrow never gets a brain
i am jealous of his candour
i know you think that makes him sweet so
in case he works this out
i keep him dumb always
the tin man is left to rust
among the talking trees
because if he gets his heart
he will fall in love with you
i cannot compete with someone
who is shiny silver and can sing
i steal the lion's medal
pin it to my shirt
the shirt i will wear each time
i visit the witch's tower
you are imprisoned here forever
i know this may appear extreme
it's just before you there was kansas
but now everything is in technicolor
and i never want you to go home.

the best christmas ever

we're watching old movies
on the new tv
your mother got you
planet of the apes
with charlton heston
the apes aren't as realistic
as the ones you see
in the new adaptations
and neither are the spaceships
but i much prefer the classics
christmas is still lingering
in that warm way it does
your reindeer lights sparkle
hung like bunting
across the bookshelf
and there is a lot of cheese left
on the wooden board
yesterday you threw our tree over
in your temper
all the baubles shattered spraying
a glass blizzard on the floor
you said i drank too much
and the gifts i got you
weren't fucking good enough
but this is still
the best christmas ever.

midnight curfew

you came like a storm
the weather readers didn't forecast
worse than galveston and harvey
bigger than a bible story
you made katrina look like drizzle
bridges split like branches
overturned trucks lay in ditches
like roadkill
the public library is now just rubble
and the city's double decker buses float
under water
like metal whales
i did not have a basement to shelter in
i didn't flee either
like the tv channels said we should
i ignored the midnight curfew
set to deter the looters
i stayed out to watch the rain pour
as the dam broke like my defences
no one could quite believe it
they had stood strong
for years
and years.

the lepidopterist and the narcissist

i will not speak of the things you do
i keep your secrets
they are like moths
with wings as thin and delicate as silk
colours
as bright as the sun
pleasing to a predator
but once swallowed
fills it with a poison that eats away
at the muscles of its heart
i caught your secrets in my net
and framed them
hung them on metal hooks on my wall
a reminder that often
the things that are the most beautiful
are the most deadly.

paraphilic infantilism

i had to buy adult nappies
i saw it on the computer
my neurologist tapped his pen on the screen
there it is
he said
so matter of fact
a scar on your spinal cord
an unusually big one
thin and long as a snake
i was angry for a while
because i'd never lost control
of anything before
this kind of thing isn't supposed to happen
to someone in their twenties
only old people shit themselves
and babies
who could ever find such a person attractive?
you said you didn't care
you loved me whatever
but still
i looked it up on the internet
there are people
who dress up like babies and fuck
i've never been into
that kind of stuff before
maybe now is a good time
to start.

madame tussauds

the two of us standing there together
grinning
my hand proudly holding yours
cameras flashing like lightning storms
kids posing in between us
while love-sick couples dreaming
of emulating our love
come and go in their thousands
then someone reaches out to touch me
and you get jealous and try to shout
but your wax lips won't move
and i can't defend myself
we earned our right to be here
with michelle and barack
william and kate
kim and kanye
i do feel for brad and angelina
who now stand in different rooms
but you always said he had his eye on me
we are not like them
when baker street station
gives way to a terrorist bomb
and when global warming is no longer a myth
the thames will burst its banks
leaving big ben tilted and rusting
on the ocean floor
but we'll still be holding hands
you crushing my crumbling clay fingers
grinning.

crab salad

when i find crabs on the beach
i'm so excited
i haven't grown up by the sea
so the only crabs i know
come in vacuum packs
processed sticks
that my mother eats in salads
there are hundreds of them
on this beach
real ones
standing in murky pools
hiding behind jagged rocks
they are dead
but they look so alive
eyes open
when i pick some from the sand
i offer them to you as tokens of my love
keepsakes of our day at the beach
i'm scared they will wake up
come alive again
snap at my face when i sleep
but still i take them
in the evening your temper rages
like a sea in a storm
something i have done
or said
wrong
i lie next to you
in the b&b double bed
eyes open
waiting for angry pincers
to get me.

cop cars

i waited outside the hospital for you
you were taking your time
and i was eyeing up the nearby toilets
in case i needed to go urgently
i'm always looking around for them
like i'm a criminal on the run
and on alert for cop cars
i watched the traffic go past in bursts
and wondered about the people inside
where they were going
to their houses after work
to dinners that have been stewing
in slow cookers
the pieces of meat tender and ready
for the kids just home from school
i wondered what kind of mother
i could be now
the kind that naps like an ageing cat
that pops pills like an addict
the kind that snaps like a letterbox
because this disease
has drained me of all my patience
and stolen my time like a criminal
who eyes up cop cars
like i eye up toilets.

**if that thing really happens when your
life flashes before your eyes**

#1

my big sister leaves for college
i cry for days on end
who will watch *jurassic park* with me now
and hide me behind a cushion?
will she ever come back?
my mother doesn't like films
she always says she's busy

#2

dad buys me a dartboard
but i can't hit the circle
my darts veer off course
like stray fireworks
i practice
as soon as i get up in the mornings
but my mother takes the dartboard down
i've ruined the wallpaper

#3

i'm special i know
because my english teacher tells me so
i'm going to go to oxford or cambridge
and my parents will be proud

#4

the day my father dies
from now on
i make the people i love leave
i banish them like traitors
no one stands a chance

#5

sixteen and pregnant
i tell lies
because it's easier than telling the truth
i won't be going to oxford or cambridge
and my parents will not be proud

#6

i leave my daughter alone in the bathtub
i only go to answer the phone
but the tap is trickling the whole time
and i find her up to her neck in bubbles

#7

meeting the perfect girl on the internet
and i've never felt so fucking lucky

#8

you used to hurt yourself
but now you like it better
hurting me
a yellow cushion off the sofa
my head smashed into
your bathroom mirror
and you blame me
you take it all back
but you can't take things like that back
ever
it's like a camera
you can't stop
the photograph from being taken
once you've pressed the button.

montauk beach

a man stopped me in the street
he was one of those god squad folk
flapping leaflets
the folk you swerve
as if they have the plague
and i have an auto immune disease so
you know
i need to be extra careful
i think he thought i was on smack
because i was only half awake
fatigue
and drugs that make me as sleepy
as a newborn baby after a feed
he told me god was here for me
here
and then i thought
of all the other places
god could be if he wanted
like yosemite national park
the grand canyon
or sitting on top
of the lighthouse on montauk beach
why would he be here
on this boarded and broken street?
and if god really was that stupid
i'd ask the bastard
why did you do this to me?

carson mccullers

on the day we first met
you waited for me in a cafe
i watched in secret
and i saw you reading a brochure
upside down
i must've looked kind of creepy
doing that
and you looked kind of crazy
with your brochure
but i was nervous
and you were just playing it cool i guess
although
i never got the impression
from your online dating profile
that you were cool
just a beautiful and lonely hunter
who had
in me
made a kill
please know
that i only ever wanted to impress you
i didn't want you to think of me
as a single mother
living with her child in a small house
crammed full of cheap furniture
cheap art
and unaccomplished ambitions
so i built myself up
brick by brick
floor by floor
and filled my building with
golden elevators
air-conditioned offices

and apartments with swimming pools
and chandeliers
until i was
in your eyes
as tall and majestic
as the empire state
i wanted you to climb me
like you were king kong
and find
at the top
a view as wow as the new york skyline
even though i knew i'd sooner or later
as if hit by an act of god
or a terrorist bomb
crumble
to the ground.

i left the valleys and moved to the city

and even the pigeons here are different
regal
their feathers are groomed and smart
their flights are purposeful
they live in the woods
only gracing this affluent
northern suburb of the city
to survey the skies
and the well-off people
below
not like
the scruffy pigeons of the valleys
they are not free
they live
in rundown sheds
in the back gardens of old men
who tie rubber rings around their ankles
and on rare occasions
let them out of wicker baskets
for racing
hoping that they will return
to the safeness of the shed
and the valleys
it's like i'm a pigeon
one of the shed ones
that somehow escaped
and now i fly around these streets
in this affluent
northern suburb of the city
with a rubber ring around my ankle
i wear one around my tongue too
that's like a tourniquet
slowly compressing my valleys accent
but one day
i will also return.

dusty springfield

we argue
over which one of us loves
dusty springfield more
and when all that is over
i lie awake listening
to the shipping forecast
with the thought of you loving dusty
more than you love me
rocking my insides
like how the ocean thrashes a buoy
on top of rough waters.

day out at the zoo

opposite our new place
there is a creepy little garden
a forgotten graveyard buried
under leaves
you get to it through rusty gates
that flake like dead skin
when you push them open
we go there sometimes
and my daughter gets excited
when she finds the graves of babies
today
beneath her adidas trainers
and worn out letters on a slab of stone
a new one
a boy
two weeks old
we eat sandwiches on a bench
and talk about death
it's cheaper
than a day out at the zoo.

the day the earth exploded

when the news channels let us know
that the asteroid was on its way to earth
doctors prescribed
everybody across the world
with pills
so that on that fateful night
we could all sleep soundly through it
but not us we went
and flushed those pills down the toilet
put on our best clothes and drove
to the top of the nearest mountain
dusty springfield crackled through the radio
and the sky lit up
and we were reckless and in love
right to the very end.

black box

the course of true love
never did run smooth
so you must find a car
well-equipped for the journey
a 4x4 with monster wheels
to make roadkill
out of those bumps in the tarmac
but us being us
we bought a private jet
and when we crashed it
you being you
parachuted out of that flaming bird
and landed in a field of candyfloss
without a scratch
the black box
containing all our secrets
and the cause of the crash
is lost
somewhere over the bermuda triangle
along with my body
i will never be found.

relapse

the nurse is cheery as she tests my eyes
so close to my face that i can smell
her breakfast
toast with marmite
but i couldn't stomach
a damn thing this morning
the letter?
o or a
i can't quite decide
letters and words are my things
i have loved them my whole life
but now i can't even do these right
they blur
a cruel joke
she pulls out a pin
i am a human voodoo doll lying
there on the bed
students watch with notepads
as i am slowly breaking down
part by part
like an old volvo
there are some things in life you wish
you could stop feeling
but your legs aren't one of them.

birds laugh

i walk the subways all the time
in the mornings there are more birds
than cars out
and in the nights
the lights fixed on the walls
are square
orange
disco balls
for the gnats who've come to party
i like the graffiti sprayed on the walls
of the concrete maze under the city
one wall says i feel fantastic
i passed it on the way back
from the hospital this morning
the birds laughed
and so did i.

national geographic channel

the polar bears are on
we used to watch them together
in high definition
on your giant smart screen telly
now i watch them alone
in my polar bear pyjama pants
because your unreasonableness
and my stubbornness
were both things as inevitable as ice
in arctic winter
if only human lives were as simple
as just needing to kill seals
to stay alive.

**they say there is always someone worse
off than you**

show them to me
because i'd like to invite them
into my apartment for a cup of tea
and an arm wrestle
to truly decide which one of us
is worse off
and if they have no arm to wrestle with
unlike me
who is lucky to have an arm
that only occasionally decides
to seize up in pain
lifeless
for a day or more
then fair enough
i'll admit defeat
and give them a prize
a biscuit to go with the tea
congratulations!
and ask them
how does it feel
stealing my thunder?

saturday night on queen street

i left my friends
drinking cocktails at the bar
they are good boys
intelligent and well dressed
they talk about books
they are the kind of friends
i longed for
as a child
but i feel like i'm bad company tonight
it's exhausting
always trying to be funny
or to say something meaningful
to say anything at all
actually
i'm sorry i have to go but
i hope you have a good
rest of the night
a guy with dreadlocks
plays drums on a bin
furiously smashing his palms down
and down
and down
like he is trying to keep up with the rain
that falls fast and hard on queen street
the burger place is rammed
i don't even remember what it's like
to be drunk and hungry
people get animalistically hungry after
drinking
and dancing
and kissing
and smoking
and fucking
don't they?
did i?

wish you were here

we were like a holiday
the best you've ever been on
off the plane
there were other holiday makers
but i didn't notice them
at the travel agents
we may as well have booked a country
all to ourselves
i got drunk on you
and the mini-bar that night
while a breeze blew through the voiles
the next morning i thumped a fist
on the tiny television set in our room
and on the news in subtitles that rolled
across the bottom of the screen it said
that a category 5 hurricane had felled
the palm trees outside the hotel
but i never noticed
you drove us to the beach in our hired car
at night
and we kissed
and more
up against the wall
the waves must've been battering behind us
but i didn't notice that either
and i was the happiest
i'd ever been in my life
i never wanted to go home
but here i am
unpacking my suitcase
and strewn in between my clothes
that smell of the ocean
are the polaroid photographs we took

they will be slotted carefully
into an album titled
memories.

the department for work and pensions

some lady from the benefit centre called over
to decide how disabled i am
i hadn't brushed my hair in days
she had clearly spent hours on hers
hi rhian how are you?
i'm just great how the fuck are you?
can you walk ten metres?
yeah but only when i'm bored of sprinting
i'm in training for the 2020 olympic games
you said on your form you have incontinence
is that right?
nah i lied
a really funny joke about being
twenty-nine years old
and planning my toilet stops
like a sight-seeing tour
you can't feel your legs sometimes?
my toes too
i know they're only small things
but please don't forget them
although you don't need a walking stick?
not yet but if i did
i would smack you in the face with it
for looking at me like that
the depression you feel
has it got any better?
oh yeah totally
i'm so fucking ecstatic being sick
and alone.

skeeter davis

i tested every bottle
in every department store in town
it had become my mission
to find your smell again
ransacking shelves and glass cabinets
on a floor as bright as heaven
a woman pressing a silver nozzle
asked me
what is the name of the perfume
you are looking for?
but the name got washed from my memory
a hundred times
like the sheets on our bed
went through the machine
i sat in the park
defeated
the park where the black statue
of john the marquess of bute
watches over the flowerbeds
the park you always said
smelled like cat piss
i never noticed it then
i was busy
absorbing you and that perfume
i resign myself to admitting
i won't ever remember the name of
i will never find that bottle
so now i guess
instead
the smell of cat piss
will always remind me of you.

two steps ahead of my friends in the recreation room

i wrote my obituary don't worry
i know that i'm not going to die
any time soon
i will outlive my enemies
and all my friends
i will watch them suffer as we grow old
two steps ahead of them
because i already know all about
the stiffness
of aching joints
all the many joys
of bladder incontinence
also totally down
with the shitting yourself stuff
and an expert at dealing with bad news
when a nurse delivers it to you
like an ugly and deformed
unwanted baby
i know what it's like to get angry at time
and feel sad about change
how it is to mourn the person you once were
and question
all of the things she did
all of the things she should've done
i will yawn in my armchair
in the recreation room of our nursing home
when greying friends are playing card games
and reminiscing.

what happens to love when it dies?

you can't give it a funeral
you can't stand up at a lectern
and tell everyone in the church how loved
love was
you can't bury it
it has no body
what happens to love when it leaves
because you can't write it a song
like joan baez who wrote *diamonds and rust*
all about her long-lost love calling her
from somewhere out in the midwest
love has no record player
there is no mobile signal where love has gone
what happens to love when it hurts you
you can't take your revenge
by lighting a bonfire
and throwing in all the photographs
you and love took
sure you could write a list
of all the things love did wrong to you
and read it over to remind yourself
that you are better off alone
but there is no reason to attempt
to put all of this in an angry letter
and send it in the mail
because love does not have a postal address
only email
love is moving on and has no time to read
your self-pity
i sent the email to love anyway
and love wrote me back
in bold and black love said
stop messaging me

mafia boss

i took classes in meditation
when i found out that memory wiping
isn't a thing
and because anger
shame
and guilt
aren't the kinds of things
you should carry around
in your back pocket
your back pocket is for your phone
that you check every minute
for texts and calls
that never come
i paid someone to teach me how to breathe
to empty my mind of everything except
the now
the silence
and the me
yeah like a mafia boss or some shit
i paid someone to get rid of you.

physio session

she pulls me about
like i am play-doh
my legs bent here
my arms twisted there
lady
can you shape me into something good?
a dinosaur
or a penguin
anything you like
just please
roll me out on the bed
thin and soft and squishy
start me all over again.

afternoon tea with a unicorn

my daughter dresses up like a unicorn
baby blue with a yellow horn
and i take her out for afternoon tea
but she is not impressed with the cakes
or the sandwiches
why are they so small?
she asks
and frowns
devouring each and every one
whoever knew unicorns
were so hard to please?
i put an adult nappy on
before we left this morning
asked her if she could see it
underneath my jeans
she got annoyed
no one will notice
it's fine
whatever mum
i suppose it is a strange sight to see
your mother wearing something that
as a baby
she would put on you
i think i embarrass her
then again
she's the one dressed up
like a fucking unicorn.

tippi hedren

thanks to the dwp
i find myself outside a miserable
brown building
on newport road
through my sunglasses it is browner still
and i bet they picked this place
on purpose
they make me walk under a flashing arch
a machine that scans me for knives
and guns
or any other weapons i may have
in my handbag
with the pills
and the nappies
i don't beep but the guy in front does
it's the metal of his wheelchair
that sets
the red alarm lights pulsing
inside a room
three judges ask me questions
they're wearing dark suits
look like crows perched on top of a wall
it's like that scene in *the birds*
where they're waiting
to peck out tippi hedren's eyes
and i try to answer them as best i can
only to be told
i am probably lying
yes i have lied a lot before
but lying is only good
when you're making yourself look cool
there is nothing cool about all of this
or me

anymore
i am on trial
but i didn't steal a car
and i never killed anybody
i'm too exhausted to even
kill myself.

indoor games

everywhere i go you are there
even though i avoid the places
i know you may be
it's as if the world is covered in sand
and your footprints are all over it
we always said we would travel
on the page of a notepad we wrote a list
of the places we wanted to visit
new york was at the very top
central park
and then on to recreate the scene
from *an affair to remember*
we couldn't die before seeing
the northern lights
and beneath them
a humpback whale in the ocean
all this from the deck
of an old battered trawler
we taught ourselves to drive
but we never even booked that cheap
all-inclusive holiday in the sun
we never left the house
instead we stayed inside every day
playing games that hurt.

the lonely hours

each day around 11 o'clock
i take the path behind
my daughter's school
a river flows alongside
and i like the family of birds
that live on it
especially the ducklings
they don't need to be apart
from their mother
for six hours a day
because she teaches them
all they need to know
these are the lonely hours
i walk by the sports field
and the school building
my daughter is somewhere inside
learning
writing
working stuff out
and no doubt worrying about her hair
and make-up
as much as i am worrying about her
is she making friends?
or missing me?
does the cute boy she likes notice her?
i bet she thinks it's pointless
having to speak welsh
i don't want her to know that i am here
passing by the windows
she would accuse me of stalking her
and die in front of her friends
if she ever saw me
i say goodbye to the ducklings

and my footsteps quicken
when i hear the distant scream
of the break-time bell.

seagulls and deckchairs and lighthouses

we were over
but i still bought you birthday gifts
i felt like i had made you up
like i was playing pretend
it was kind of crazy
shopping for things i knew
i'd never give you
i went for a seaside theme
i thought you'd like that so i picked
an antique nautical compass
those chocolate seashells in a box
sylvanian families with buckets
and spades
a ship in a bottle
the birthday card had on the front
an image
of a busy beach somewhere in england
back in the 60s
on the day itself i wrapped the gifts
in paper that was thick and blue
it had seagulls
and deckchairs
and lighthouses
all over it
even though i knew you were somewhere
eating cake with someone else.

letter to my brain

i write to you
as if you are a childhood friend
i lost touch with
hey
what happened?
we used to be cool
me and you
you kept all my secrets in your neurons
like a safe deposit box
and together we were top of the class
talented
our teacher said
we had an aptitude for words
and ahead of us lay
a future as bright as the lights
on the christmas tree
at rockefeller center
but now you are a stranger
you turned against me
it's like you made a promise
with your fingers crossed.

letter to my daughter

most of all
i hope you will be happy
but i hope you will also be smart
be careful
be brave
ride
on the biggest rollercoaster at the fair
don't take drugs
except for your vitamin d
drive a nice car
but be environmentally friendly
travel the world
don't stay where you are
swim seas and climb mountains
go to yosemite and the grand canyon
anywhere and everywhere you want
don't forget to call me though
to tell me all about it
always call me
fall in love
but be their wallis simpson
find someone
who would give up everything for you
and when you've done all that
i hope you will look after me
when i need you
the way i looked after you
when you had your tonsils out
you even had a bell to ring when you wanted
ice cubes
and snacks
so don't you forget that fucking bell
but i'll try not to need you
for a long time yet.

i want to be a shooting star

i don't want to end up in a wheelchair
i don't want to read of the death
of joan baez
on bbc news
i don't want to lose my sight
how could i write
and how could i stare at the moon
and stars in the sky
or watch porn
the sounds are great
but that's not enough for me
i like to see what they're all doing
i don't want to forget you
i don't want to ever not remember
the second date we had
on the back seats of your car
there was no sex
just dusty springfield on your stereo
and i held you so close it was perfect
i thought i'd always be holding you
on the back seats of cars
at the theatre
on the megabus
down at the lake
with the moorhens and the lighthouse
i don't want to answer the call from my nurse
it's probably bad news
i don't want my daughter to grow up
i'm scared she'll hate me when she learns
of all the mistakes i made when i was young
i don't want to meditate today
i'll just fall asleep
my therapist will be mad

but i'll tell her i have anyway
i'm totally at one with myself
and calm
those bad thoughts are under control i swear
i don't want to die young
despite always saying i'd love to do that
signing off in style before i burn out
like marc bolan
mama cass
and otis redding
i thought that was cool
but now i just want to live
like a shooting star
i want to burn on
and on.

the last polar bear on earth

the cat has noticed you are gone
she walks the empty half of the bed
like she is the last polar bear on earth
making her way across a vast
and endless ice cap
stamping on your pillow and shifting
from one paw to the other
one paw to the other
she asks sadly
where is the other human
who used to lay here?
i liked her
she made the bed warm
the cat misses you.

pink woollen hat

i can't wait for winter
in my new hometown
christmas will make me sad
but the church will look so pretty
covered in snow
the streets will remember me
when i print my footsteps
on their frozen stones
my daughter's eyes
will look even bluer in the cold
but she will not want to wear
her pink woollen hat
she will throw her mittens in protest
to the floor
i'm told it's not cool
to keep warm
anymore.

christmas presents

i was moving on although
i admit
not even ten minutes went by
without thinking about you
but i was happy knowing
that there would never again be
another christmas
where you'd wrap presents like
stupid
useless
selfish
loser
whore
slut
and lovingly give them to me
then came the apologies
the promises to change
and i thought of all the nice presents
you'd ever given me like
the wolf pocket watch
the locket
the coffee machine
the dark green fountain pen
but in the end your only concern was
that i'd keep
my mouth
shut
so i went and took all your presents
down to the local charity shop
someone less fortunate than me
is more than welcome to them now.

god orders room service

an extra-large bed
greets me
when i use the keycard to open the door
i'll sleep in it alone tonight
i've never stayed in a hotel room
by myself before now
i'm not a business man
in the city to attend a conference
i'm not a lone traveller
looking to find myself in a brand new
and beautiful place
i'm not a hotel inspector
here to find stains on mattresses
or to check
that the towels in the bathroom
are fresh
and folded
the way five-star hotels are expected
to fold their towels
i'm not god
i like to think that if he exists
he's not high up in the clouds
but down here
undercover
travelling from place to place
disguised as a businessman
or a lone traveller
looking to find himself on earth
living out of hotel rooms he's got
an endless supply of money so
he orders room service each night
from his extra-large bed
showers

and dries himself off with towels that
are fresh
and folded
the way hotel inspectors say
five-star hotels should fold them
i'm not god anyway
maybe he doesn't mind
sleeping alone.

the morning the huge tree got uprooted

from my bedroom window i watched
as the wind tore it out of the ground
as easily as a kid plucks
a dandelion
from the soil
i had an appointment with my therapist
and i told her how i thought the tree
was symbolic
the tree is me
i told her
because i once knew who i was
where i belonged
i had a purpose
and i thought i was steady
and strong
but then you came
and went
and just like the wind blew the huge tree up
and out of the ground
and into the metal fence
you uprooted me
the council put up some tape
a barrier to keep the kids from climbing
people stop in their tracks
to take photos on their phones
of the tree
that flew through the air
and my best friend says not to worry
i will re-grow
one day
and be gloriously blown away
again.

backstrokers

in that drunken blackout
my mind froze like an old computer
and when it turned back on
i was sure someone had hurt me
the way you did
we all come to the water
for different reasons
i don't know theirs
but every morning we are the same people
sporting
different coloured spandex
in this giant square of shimmering
blue
separated by lanes
according to your speed
in the fast one the serious swimmers
wear hats
check their times on watches as they're
thrashing back and forth
making waves
angry white froth
that spits and spills over
into the middle lane
where people kick at a medium
civilised
pace
they're getting annoyed
at the backstrokers
who have absolutely no consideration
for who may be in front of them
then in the slow lane there's me
and the chinese ladies
who do not swim at all
they just walk around in the water

like they're wading through treacle
laughing hysterically
and speaking words i do not understand
they wish me good morning though
every day
and i do the same
because courtesy is a language
everyone speaks in the water
everyone besides
the backstrokers.

panic/shark attack

i am swimming my way out of this
it's funny
how i catch my breath back in the water
it's supposed to be the other way around
a human being can only hold its breath
under water
for approximately two minutes
but down here that burning
rushing
feeling
is lifted off my chest
flashbacks of violence
and the screams
of cruel names become
inaudible echoes
like the whistles
lifeguards blow
high up on their chairs
and i chase the bad thoughts away
like they are tiny fish
and i am a huge and hungry shark
i don't even care if in the changing room
the other women see my vagina
that i haven't shaved in months
they can look at it if they want.

2017

the year we all forgot
to hold our breaths and wait
for the next celebrity to die
because terrorists were busy
blowing up those kids
who were watching their favourite singer
dance in the arena
the year a building as tall as the sky
kept the poor people hidden
out of sight of their rich neighbours
next door
and caught fire
mothers dropped their babies
out of smoky windows
and some guy from syria had crossed
the ocean
to live
peacefully there
only to burn alive
because poor people aren't worthy
of fire safety regulations
the year i realised that love is a window
low enough to jump out of
and that this disease is not an ocean
it is only a puddle i have to
step over.

MS

when the shock and the anger goes
when you have neatly organised
all your pills into daily boxes
and made your peace with those two letters
that will follow you around
for the rest of your life
like a stalker
you realise you are still the same person
no one read that poem
the one you always wanted read
at your funeral
the one by larkin
not the really famous one
the one about the dream he has
of someone he used to know
and how the things he'd forgotten about them
come back to him
like letters to someone who left the house
years ago
no one read it because you never died
in fact
perhaps
this is your chance to start over again.

Thanks a lot to Parthian for making this book and to all the editors who have included some of these poems in their publications. I'm very grateful to Susie Wild, Rebecca Parfitt, Fizzy Oppe, Crystal Jeans, Catrin Kean, clare e. potter, Tiffany Murray, Rhys Owain Williams, Jonathan Edwards, Siôn Tomos Owen and Richard Davies. And I'm very thankful to the crazy bunch of people who are the Hay Festival Writers at Work, for the friendship and inspiration that has followed since we all got together.

Discover new writing with Parthian